SUCCESS

ACKNOWLEDGMENTS

To Jack Stockman
of Oak Park, Illinois,
for the art work
on the cover.

To Erika Tiepel
of Littleton, Colorado,
for the layout
and design.

To Zondervan Bible Publishers
for permission to use the
Holy Bible: New International Version

©1973, 1978, 1984 by International Bible Society.
Used by permission of Zondervan Bible Publishers.

SUCCESS

DOES THE ONE WITH THE MOST TOYS WIN?

PETER MENCONI, RICHARD PEACE,
& LYMAN COLEMAN

DEVELOPED BY
SERENDIPITY
H O U S E

DISTRIBUTED BY
NAVPRESS®
A MINISTRY OF THE NAVIGATORS

© 1988, Serendipity House. All rights reserved.

QUESTIONS ABOUT THIS COURSE FOR AN

ENTRY LEVEL SUPPORT GROUP

PURPOSE

1. **What is this course all about?** Becoming a support group while studying the Bible.

SEEKERS/ STRUGGLERS

2. **Who is it for?** Two kinds of people: (a) Seekers who do not know where they are with God but are open to finding out, and (b) Strugglers who are committed to Jesus Christ but need to grow in their faith.

BABY BOOMERS

3. **Who is this course specifically designed for?** While the course is for everyone, the series is primarily written for Baby Boomers.

NEW PEOPLE

4. **Does this mean that I can invite my "non-church" friends?** Absolutely, this is what this group is all about—giving people a chance to restart their spiritual pilgrimage.

STUDY

5. **What are we going to study?** Six definitions of "success" (see inside front cover) and what the Bible has to say about each one.

AUTHORS

6. **Who wrote the material?** Peter Menconi (dentist/consultant/free-lance writer), Richard Peace (seminary professor and free-lance consultant on media), and Lyman Coleman (group process trainer and writer).

DREAM

7. **What motivated them to write this course?** A dream to offer to Baby Boomers and others the chance to investigate the Christian life for a few weeks in a support group.

FIRST SESSION

8. **What do we do at the meetings?** In the first session, you get acquainted and decide on one of two Bible study tracks. In sessions two through seven, you follow the track you chose.

TWO TRACKS

9. **What are the two tracks?** Gospel Study or Epistle Study. The Gospel Study is a more basic, "entry-level" study with a questionnaire with multiple choice options. (None of the options are "right" or "wrong." They are designed to start you thinking.) The Epistle Study has open-ended questions that usually necessitate more involvement in the Scripture text.

CHOOSING

10. Which track of Bible Study do you recommend? The Gospel Study is best for newly-formed groups or groups that are unfamiliar with small group Bible study. The Epistle Study is best for deeper Bible study groups.

BOTH

11. Can you choose both? Yes, depending upon your time schedule.

Here's how to decide:

STUDY	APPROXIMATE COMPLETION TIME
Gospel Study only	40-60 minutes
Epistle Study only	40-60 minutes
Gospel and Epistle Study	80-120 minutes

HOMEWORK OPTION

12. What if we want to do both the Gospel and Epistle Studies but don't have time at the session? You can spend two weeks on a unit—the Gospel Study the first week and the Epistle Study the next. Or, you can do the Gospel Study in the session and the Epistle Study for homework.

BIBLE KNOWLEDGE

13. What if you don't know anything about the Bible? No problem. The Gospel Study is based on a parable or story that stands on its own—to discuss as though you are hearing it for the first time. The Epistle Study comes with complete Reference Notes—to keep you up to speed.

THE FEARLESS FOURSOME

HOW TO OVERCOME GROUP JITTERS!

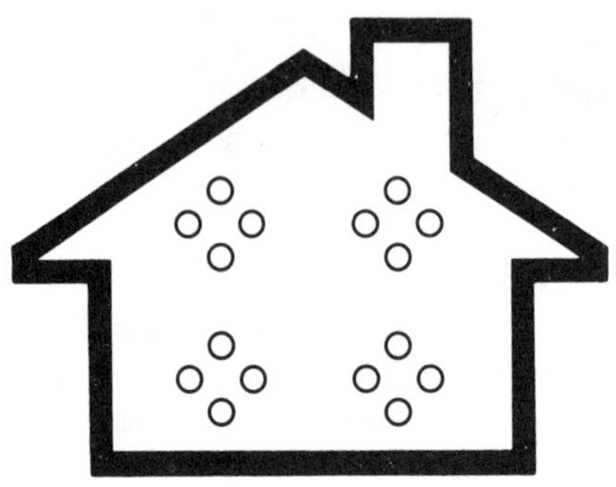

PROBLEM: A lot of people are afraid of groups.

SOLUTION: Divide into groups of 4 when the time comes for sharing. In 4's the quiet person will be able to talk, and the talkative person will not dominate as much. In fact, in 4's most of the problems of group dynamics will be avoided.

SO: When the time comes for sharing, ask 4 to sit around the dining table, 4 around the kitchen table, and 4 around a folding table in the family room.

REFERENCE NOTES

14. What is the purpose of the Reference Notes in the Epistle Study? To help you understand the context of the Bible passage and any difficult words that need to be defined.

LEADERSHIP

15. Who leads the meetings? One person can lead for the whole time—or you can rotate the leadership.

RULES

16. What are the ground rules for the group?

- ☐ Priority: While you are in the course, you give the group meetings priority.
- ☐ Participation: Everyone participates and no one dominates.
- ☐ Respect: Everyone is given the right to their own opinion and "dumb questions" are encouraged and respected.
- ☐ Confidentiality: Anything that is said in the meeting is never repeated outside the meeting.
- ☐ Empty Chair: The group stays open to new people at every meeting as long as they understand the ground rules.
- ☐ Support: Permission is given to call upon each other in time of need —even in the middle of the night.

CONTINUING

17. What happens to the group after finishing the course? The group is free to disband or continue to another course.

SESSION 1
Introduction

Success is an elusive commodity. It is pursued by many, but achieved by few. But what is true success? Success is defined in numerous ways in our society. To some, success is seen as the power of a Wall Street "mover and shaker" or wealth of a TV superstar. Or success may be the status lavished on the winner of an Oscar or Olympic gold medal. Still others see success as the achievement of happiness or self-fulfillment.

As you move through the following group studies, you will be interacting with your group and the Bible on the varying dimensions of success. With a little help from your friends, you should more clearly understand what constitutes true success. Enjoy!

FYI

For Your Information

- The average salary for *Fortune* 1,000 CEOs is over $500,000/year.
- According to a survey by *INC.* and *USA Today*, the young executives who run the fastest-growing private companies in America are predominately male, white, Protestant, and Republican.
- The actor Marlon Brando is said to have collected a fee of $3.7 million, plus $15 million in profit percentages, for a mere 12 days' work in the 1978 film *Superman*—a rate of more than $1,500,000 a day.
- . . . half of those considered successful by their peers are unhappy.

Dr. Douglas LaBier, quoted
in *U.S. News and World Report*

LEADER: IF YOU HAVE MORE THAN SEVEN PEOPLE AT THE MEETING, SUBDIVIDE INTO GROUPS OF FOUR FOR SHARING (SEE BOX ON PAGE 6).

Orientation: In the first session, take some time to review the questions and answers on pages 5-7 about this course, especially the RULES for a support group under question 16.

OPEN

STEP ONE: Answer the following questions and share your responses with the group.

1. When you were growing up, what was your idea of success?
   a. Popularity with the opposite sex; making it with a certain someone
   b. Making the best grades; getting into the best school
   c. Escaping the unhappy situations I saw around me; finding happiness
   d. Being elected class president/team captain; presiding over others
   e. Getting other people to do my bidding; getting my needs met
   f. Becoming independent of mom or dad; paying your own way

2. What kind of person did your high school senior class elect as "Most Likely to Succeed"? What standards were used to define success? Where is that person now?

3. Which of the following do you feel are the most common ways people pursue happiness? (Choose two.)
   a. By achieving social status
   b. By having a loving family and friends
   c. By acquiring knowledge
   d. By getting rich
   e. By serving others
   f. By living in harmony with nature
   g. By pursuing their spiritual beliefs
   h. By achieving successful careers
   i. By maintaining good health

4. Which of the following do you think offers the best definition of "self-fulfillment"?
   a. Self-fulfillment is not having any wants and desires
   b. Self-fulfillment is being at peace with yourself
   c. Self-fulfillment is having a job you really love
   d. Self-fulfillment is being loved
   e. Self-fulfillment is using your abilities to the fullest

5. Which of the following best exemplifies a life of service?
   a. Being a doctor or nurse in an inner-city clinic
   b. Being a mother or father
   c. Being a missionary in Outer Zambezi
   d. Being a true friend
   e. Being a Peace Corps volunteer
   f. Being a dedicated employee

STUDY

STEP TWO: This exercise will help introduce you to the topics of the remaining six sessions. Answer the following questions and discuss your responses with your group.

1. Judging from your calendar, your checkbook, and the unsolicited testimony of others who know you, what is your idea of success—now that you have "grown up"?
   a. Climbing the corporate, military or political ladder; wielding power over others
   b. Climbing the golf, tennis or racquetball ladder; beating the competition
   c. Becoming independently wealthy; able to retire early
   d. Belonging to the club of __________ ; having friends who __________
   e. Escaping the unhappy situations I see around me; finding happiness
   f. Popularity with the opposite sex; making it with a certain someone
   g. Gaining all the knowledge you can in your chosen field of endeavor; going on for advanced study or more degrees
   h. Staying out of debt, out of trouble, out of jail, out of the hospital

2. Judging by what you do with your discretionary time and money, what award, honor or office are you seeking?
   a. "Dad/Mom of the Year" (popularity with your kids)
   b. "Volunteer of the Year" (satisfying your need to be needed)
   c. "President of __________ " (earning the respect of your colleagues)
   d. "Employee of the Month"—more than once (earning peer respect)
   e. "Patron Saint" (out-giving others in the roll of donors to your favorite charity)
   f. "Fan of the Year" (awarded by your favorite team or hero)
   g. "Alumni of the Year" (for outstanding service to your alma mater)
   h. " __________'s Hall of Fame" (for achievements in your favorite sport)
   i. "Degree in __________" (for academic achievement in your specialty)
   j. Oscar, Emmy or Grammy award for your acting or musical ability
   k. Winner of the Nobel Prize in __________ (for your activist efforts in that cause you have dedicated yourself to)

REFLECT

STEP THREE: As time allows, discuss with your group your agreement or disagreement with the following statements.

- Try not to become a man of success but rather try to become a man of value. *— Albert Einstein*

- Let us work as if success depended upon ourselves alone; but with heartfelt conviction that we are doing nothing and God everything. *— St. Ignatius Loyola*

SESSION 2
Success as Power

The acquisition and use of power has motivated people throughout the centuries. In the past several decades, many of us have witnessed the rise and fall of Student Power, Black Power, Gray Power, and Power to the People. We have been fascinated by the use and abuse of power on popular TV shows such as *Dallas, Dynasty,* and *LA Law.* And we have been sickened by the real-life abuses of power in the Watergate and Iran-Contra affairs.

Power is a curious thing. It can be abused certainly. But it can also be used for good. Jesus exemplified the constructive and compassionate use of power when he healed people physically, emotionally, and spiritually.

But what is power really, at its root? Domination over others? The skill of making things happen? Force that cannot be resisted? The ability to effect miracles? The secular view of power has to do largely with the idea of dominance. The New Testament view of power is quite different. It involves action that springs from a place of weakness, not from a place of superiority.

You will have a chance to see this demonstrated in the Gospel Study in the life of Jesus, and to study the Biblical principle which underlies this in the Epistle Study from 1 Corinthians. As you work through these two passages ask yourself constantly: who is the successful person in God's view.

OPTION 1

Gospel Study/Power Struggle

OPEN

STEP ONE: Answer the following questions and share your responses with your group.

LEADER: IF YOU HAVE MORE THAN SEVEN AT THE MEETING, SUBDIVIDE INTO GROUPS OF FOUR FOR GREATER PARTICIPATION (SEE BOX ON PAGE 6).

1. When you were a teenager, who had the most power over your life, or whose message did you find irresistible? (Check two)

___ your mother/father
___ your grandparents
___ your sister/brother
___ a minister/youth leader
___ a school teacher
___ a close neighbor
___ a same-sex friend
___ an opposite-sex friend
___ a TV/movie star
___ an athlete/coach

2. Complete this sentence for your situation: "If only I were my own boss, I would then be able to ______________________________."

STUDY

STEP TWO: Read Matthew 4:1-11 and discuss your response to the following questions with your group.

1Then Jesus was led by the Spirit into the desert to be tempted by
the devil. 2After fasting forty days and forty nights, he was hungry.
3The tempter came to him and said, "If you are the Son of God, tell
these stones to become bread."
4Jesus answered, "It is written: 'Man does not live on bread alone,
but on every word that comes from the mouth of God.' "
5Then the devil took him to the holy city and had him stand on the
highest point of the temple. 6"If you are the Son of God," he said,
"throw yourself down. For it is written: " ' He will command his angels
concerning you, and they will lift you up in their hands, so that you
will not strike your foot against a stone.' "
7Jesus answered him, "It is also written: 'Do not put the Lord your
God to the test.' "
8Again, the devil took him to a very high mountain and showed
him all the kingdoms of the world and their splendor.
9"All this I will give you," he said, "if you will bow down and
worship me."
10Jesus said to him, "Away from me, Satan! For it is written:
'Worship the Lord your God, and serve him only.' "
11Then the devil left him, and angels came and attended him.

Matthew 4:1-11 NIV

1. Would you say you "eat to live" or you "live to eat"? What is the longest you have been without food? What were the circumstances?

2. How would you describe the power struggle going on here?
  a. This is the classic struggle between good and evil
  b. Satan is trying to conquer Jesus when he seems weak and powerless
  c. This power struggle is no different than the ones we face daily
  d. Satan is trying to conquer Jesus by tempting him on the physical, intellectual, emotional, and spiritual levels

3. What was the devil attempting to do with Jesus?
  a. He was trying to physically kill Jesus
  b. He was trying to play "mind games" with Jesus
  c. He was trying to get Jesus to worship him
  d. He was trying to enlist Jesus as an ally

4. What tactics did Jesus use to counter Satan?
   a. He called on an army of angels to help him
   b. He quoted Old Testament Scripture as authoritative rebuttals
   c. He changed the subject
   d. He appealed to a higher authority or power
   e. He told Satan to "Beat it!"

5. In verse 3, why did the devil challenge Jesus to change stones into bread?
   a. He wanted to see if Jesus could really do it
   b. He wanted to exercise some control over Jesus
   c. He was mocking and daring Jesus
   d. He knew Jesus was very hungry and vulnerable

6. In these verses, what do you learn about Satan?
   a. He also knows and can quote Scripture
   b. He is able to change his tactics as circumstances dictate
   c. He is easily frustrated
   d. He tries to tempt at a point of weakness

7. What can be learned from the way Jesus handled this power struggle?
   a. That even in a moment of weakness, we should fight back
   b. That power is exerted with the "Big Picture" in mind
   c. That power struggles should be avoided at all cost
   d. That power can be used without annihilating others
   e. That God is ultimately in control

APPLY

STEP THREE: Select ONE of the following scenarios and discuss your response with your group.

1. You were just elected President of the United States. As the most powerful person in the Free World, you wield awesome power. You can start World War III or pursue nuclear disarmament. You can initiate domestic policies which can make the rich richer and the poor poorer. Or, you can give leadership to the elimination of poverty, illiteracy and racism. How will you use your newly-acquired power?

2. You have just taken over as president of OPEC (Organization of Petroleum Exporting Countries). You now have power over most of the world's oil supply. You can determine which countries will have enough oil and which countries will not. By directly affecting the economies of these countries, you can shift the balance of world power. How will you use your newly-acquired power?

3. You have just been "kicked up" to become president of NBC. You will now have a major influence over what kind of television shows will be aired on your network. You will have significant control over all entertainment, news, and sports programming. In fact, you have almost been given a forum for your personal agenda. How will you use this newly-acquired power?

OPTION 2

Epistle Study/Power Grab

OPEN

STEP ONE: Start with the OPEN questions on page 11.

STUDY

STEP TWO: Read 1 Corinthians 1:18–2:5 below and discuss the questions on the next page with your group. If you do not understand a word or phrase, check the Reference Notes page 16.

18For the message of the cross is foolishness to those who are
perishing, but to us who are being saved it is the power of God. 19For
it is written:
"I will destroy the wisdom of the wise; the intelligence of the
intelligent I will frustrate."
20Where is the wise man? Where is the scholar? Where is the
philosopher of this age? Has not God made foolish the wisdom of the
world? 21For since in the wisdom of God the world through its wisdom
did not know him, God was pleased through the foolishness of what
was preached to save those who believe. 22Jews demand miraculous
signs and Greeks look for wisdom, 23but we preach Christ crucified: a
stumbling block to Jews and foolishness to Gentiles, 24but to those
whom God has called, both Jews and Greeks, Christ the power of God
and the wisdom of God. 25For the foolishness of God is wiser than
man's wisdom, and the weakness of God is stronger than man's
strength.
26Brothers, think of what you were when you were called. Not
many of you were wise by human standards; not many were
influential; not many were of noble birth. 27But God chose the foolish
things of the world to shame the wise; God chose the weak things of
the world to shame the strong. 28He chose the lowly things of this
world and the despised things—and the things that are not—to nullify
the things that are, 29so that no one may boast before him. 30It is
because of him that you are in Christ Jesus, who has become for us
wisdom from God—that is, our righteousness, holiness and
redemption. 31Therefore, as it is written: "Let him who boasts boast in
the Lord."

[1]When I came to you, brothers, I did not come with eloquence or superior wisdom as I proclaimed to you the testimony about God. [2]For I resolved to know nothing while I was with you except Jesus Christ and him crucified. [3]I came to you in weakness and fear, and with much trembling. [4]My message and my preaching were not with wise and persuasive words, but with a demonstration of the Spirit's power, [5]so that your faith might not rest on men's wisdom, but on God's power.

I Corinthians 1:18–2:5 NIV

1. Where would you look for true wisdom? For true power?

2. In what way is the message of the cross related to the power of God?

3. What is meant by the statement that "the foolishness of God is wiser than man's wisdom"?

4. What is meant by the statement that "the weakness of God is stronger than man's strength"?

5. Why has God chosen the weak and lowly to communicate his truth?

6. What motivated the Apostle Paul to preach as he did?

7. According to Paul, what power is at the disposal of all Christians?

8. Do you think Paul viewed his ministry as a success? If so, why? If not, why not?

REFLECT

STEP THREE: As time allows, discuss with your group your agreement or disagreement with the following statements.

- Power undirected by high purpose spells calamity; and high purpose by itself is utterly useless if the power to put it into effect is lacking.

  — *Theodore Roosevelt*

- Real power in prayer flows only when man's spirit touches God's spirit.

  — *Catherine Marshall*

APPLY

STEP FOUR: Answer the following questions and share your responses with the group.

1. What modern advertizing slogan best fits your values regarding power?
   a. "Oh, what a feeling!" (Toyota)
   b. "Just one look. That's all it took." (Mazda)
   c. "Let the good times roll." (Kawasaki)
   d. "Think small." (Volkswagen)
   e. "Life is too short not to go first class." (Mercedes-Benz)

2. How would you compare your own idea of wisdom and power: more like the secular world . . . or more like Paul in this passage?

3. Are you more likely to abuse the power you have been given at home or at work? With those you dearly love, or with those you hardly know?

REFERENCE NOTES

Summary: The fact that the Corinthians can boast of party slogans is a clear indication that they overvalue human wisdom and misunderstand the nature of the gospel. In the light of this Paul explains in verses 18–25 the difference between human and divine wisdom. He shows that the gospel is decidedly not a specie of human philosophy—because it involves such a reversal of human expectation. Who would have thought that God would work through the scandal of the cross? Only God could demonstrate his power through a dying, powerless "criminal." Paul then goes on to "prove" that God does indeed work through weakness. He first looks at the Corinthians (verses 26–31) and then at himself (2:1–5), pointing out that they were not very clever and he was not very persuasive, so the fact they are Christians "proves" that God works through weakness. How else could the fact of the church at Corinth be explained?

v. 18 **the message of the cross . . .** This is the only legitimate slogan. Paul immediately puts the issue in stark terms: the question of eternal destiny hinges upon the meaning of the cross. Their misunderstanding and the resultant division is no slight matter. It strikes at the core of the gospel.

foolishness . . . It is absurd to many that at the center of God's redemptive activity lies death by crucifixion. Note that the opposite of *foolishness* is not *wisdom,* but (God's) *power.*

being saved . . . Salvation is a process, begun at conversion, consummated at the Second Coming, and fulfilled in eternity.

v. 20 **. . .** All those who represent human wisdom are forced to flee in the face of God's revelation that their wisdom is actually mere folly.

v. 21 **. . .** The wisdom of God "is not a plan that men would ever have thought of because it operates through Christian preaching which, since it is focused upon the cross (v. 18) will inevitably be judged by worldly standards to be not wisdom but folly" (Barrett).

v. 22 **Jews demand miraculous signs . . .** The Jews expected a Messiah who would come in obvious power doing miraculous deeds. In Jesus they saw one so weak that his enemies got away with killing him. "To the Jew, a crucified Messiah was an impossible contradiction, like 'cooked ice' " (Fee). The Jews demanded that God certify his activity by means of supernatural acts.

Greeks look for wisdom . . . Their delight was in clever, cunning logic delivered with soaring persuasiveness. The idea that a Jewish peasant who died as a convicted criminal could be the focus of God's redemptive plan for the world was so silly as to be laughable.

v. 23 **. . .** To accept the word of the cross is to accept that we as people are weak, sinful, and helpless before God. It is to accept that we cannot understand God on our own nor devise ways to reach him by ourselves. We must trust God, not our human wisdom and power, and this is a scandal to many.

stumbling block . . . Literally, "a scandal." Jesus' crucifixion "proved" that he could not be of God since according to Deuteronomy 21:23, those hanging from a tree are cursed of God. A suffering, dying Messiah was totally outside first-century Jewish expectation.

foolishness . . . Both the incarnation and the crucifixion were totally unexpected. The Greeks felt that gods would not act like that. In fact, the cradle and the cross show that people cannot reach God via the route of wisdom and reason but only by the response of faith to that which has been done for them.

v. 24 **. . .** In fact, Christ is indeed both the sign that is craved by the Jews (he is the power of God) and the ultimate truth desired by the Greeks (he is the wisdom of God).

v. 25 **. . .** There is indeed a paradox at the heart of the gospel, at least when the gospel is viewed through the lens of human wisdom. But in actual fact Christ crucified conveys the truth about God and provides the power to break human bondage.

v. 26 **think of what you were . . .** In fact, in their own calling one sees this same paradox: the all-powerful God using the "weak things of the world."

not many . . . The early church had special appeal to the poor and to those with little social standing. This was part of its offensiveness to the culture in general. The "wrong" people were attracted to it. On the other hand, it is clear that there were some influential people in the Corinthian Church. For example, there was Crispus, a former head of the synagogue who had a position of status in the Jewish community (Acts 18:8), and there was Erastus, who as director of public works in Corinth, was a man of wealth and power (Romans 16:23).

v. 27 **the foolish things of the world . . .** Those who in the *estimation of the current culture* were insignificant.

to shame . . . By proving that the wise men were, in fact, quite wrong.

v. 29 **. . .** A church composed of such folk ought to have a better grasp of what the gospel is all about because they would know that it was not on account of who they were or what they had done, that they were chosen. There ought to be, therefore, no false boasting within the church. To *boast* is to wrongly evaluate one's own gifts, put confidence in them, and to express this with a tinge of pride. Such boasting was one of the problems in the Corinthian church.

v. 30 **because of him . . .** They owe the fact that they are related to God solely to Jesus Christ.

wisdom from God . . . Paul spoke of "human wisdom" in verse 17, i.e., philosophical wisdom. But here he begins to "de-philosophize" *sophia* (wisdom) and instead historicize it. The historical Jesus, not some philosophical proposition, is God's wisdom. It is Christ who mediates God's plan of salvation. *Righteousness, holiness,* and *redemption* are three of Paul's metaphors for salvation.

righteousness . . . Christ is *our righteousness* in that he took upon himself the guilt of human sin. So on the Last Day when Christians stand before the Judge, they are viewed not in terms of their own failure and inadequacy but as being "in Christ." Thus his righteousness assures them of acquittal.

holiness . . . Human beings cannot come before a Holy God because they are not holy; but once again Christ provides what people lack. His holiness suffices for them and so a relationship with God is assured.

redemption . . . It is by Christ's redeeming work on the cross that wisdom, righteousness and holiness are mediated to humankind.

2:1-5 . . . Paul shows that, in fact, his own ministry amongst them was a demonstration of the principles outlined in 1:18-31.

v. 1 **eloquence or superior wisdom . . .** "The two nouns are close together in meaning, for *eloquence* (literally, logos *or 'word'*) here is rational talk, and *wisdom* worldly cleverness. They represent the outward and inward means by which men may commend a case, effectiveness of language, and skill of argumentation" (Barrett).

v. 2 . . . In Corinth, a city teeming with articulate philosophers, Paul's refusal to make persuasive speech and brilliant logic preeminent in his evangelism was especially striking. Instead he simply preached (not "orated") the crucified Christ (a paradox to most).

v. 3 . . . Not for his own safety but because of the awesome responsibility he had as a preacher of the gospel.

v. 4 . . . Paul says he was not an impressive speaker (2 Corinthians 10:1), even though his writing (which was spoken to a scribe and has the "feel" of speech) is often quite eloquent. As E. Norden wrote: "In these passages (Romans 8 and 1 Corinthians 13) the diction of the Apostle rises to the height of Plato's in the *Phaedrus.*"

demonstration of the Spirit's power . . . Paul here reveals the secret behind the impact that his preaching made. People were moved, not by his human eloquence, but by the inner, convicting power of the Holy Spirit. This is the real proof of the validity of the gospel.

SESSION 3
Success as Wealth

Wealth—how to get it, how to use it, how to keep it—probably consumes more time and energy than any other human endeavor. We never seem to have enough money or material goods. And many of us feel that all our problems would be solved if we were only rich. Or as someone once said, "If money can't buy happiness, at least it can buy off unhappiness."

Amassing wealth has become almost a game for some. It is not even the money that matters so much; money is simply a way of keeping track of who is ahead. Money becomes a way of measuring success and success becomes a way of feeling good.

While wealth is not inherently wrong, it brings greater responsibility and peril to those who want to follow Christ. Wealth, like power, can be either positively used or destructively abused. As we will see in the following studies, both Jesus and Paul understood the "upside and downside" of wealth.

OPTION 1

Gospel Study/Money Talks

OPEN

STEP ONE: Answer the following questions and share your responses with your group.

LEADER: IF YOU HAVE MORE THAN SEVEN IN THE GROUP, SUBDIVIDE INTO GROUPS OF FOUR FOR GREATER PARTICIPATION (SEE BOX ON PAGE 6).

1. When you were 18 years old, what was your idea of wealth?
   a. Start your own business and keep it going, independent of parents
   b. Play the field, enjoy many boy/girl relationships
   c. Get married, buy a house, raise a family, own lots of "goodies"
   d. Get through college, get a job—anything to get out of the house
   e. A growing relationship with God
   f. "To see the USA in your new Corvette Chevrolet"
   g. Good health and peace of mind
   h. $1,000,000 in the bank by the time you are 30

2. By age 30, which of these had you (or will you have) attained? What other signs of wealth have you accumulated along the way?

STUDY

STEP TWO: Read Luke 12:13-21 and discuss your response to the following questions with your group.

13Someone in the crowd said to him, "Teacher, tell my brother to divide the inheritance with me."

14Jesus replied, "Man, who appointed me a judge or an arbiter between you?" 15Then he said to them, "Watch out! Be on your guard against all kinds of greed; a man's life does not consist in the abundance of his possessions."

16And he told them this parable: "The ground of a certain rich man produced a good crop. 17He thought to himself, 'What shall I do? I have no place to store my crops.' "

18"Then he said, 'This is what I'll do. I will tear down my barns and build bigger ones, and there I will store all my grain and my goods. 19And I'll say to myself, "You have plenty of good things laid up for many years. Take life easy; eat, drink and be merry." '

20"But God said to him, 'You fool! This very night your life will be demanded from you. Then who will get what you have prepared for yourself?'

21"This is how it will be with anyone who stores up things for himself but is not rich toward God."

Luke 12:13-21 NIV

1. As you understand "wealth," would you say your family is now *more* wealthy, or *less* wealthy, than the previous generation? Why?

2. In verse 13, what was the man in the crowd really saying to Jesus?
   a. My brother is treating me poorly
   b. I want my share of the action
   c. Would you straighten out this mess
   d. My brother is greedy
   e. What does the Jewish law say about inheritance?

3. In his reply, what was Jesus telling the crowd?
   a. Greed will get you into trouble
   b. I am not a judge
   c. Money, wealth, and material goods are not important
   d. Concern for money and wealth can easily get out of control

4. In this parable, what is Jesus saying about wealth and the pursuit of wealth?
   a. Wealth will make us better people
   b. Wealth can make us greedy
   c. Wealth can be used to further the Kingdom of God
   d. Wealth can make us self-indulgent

5. In what ways are the thoughts and actions of the rich man similar to present-day behavior?
   a. We (our society) place a high priority on security
   b. We think "bigger is better"
   c. We use our money and resources wisely
   d. We want to have it all
   e. We feel that if we have more wealth, we are better people

6. Why is God's response to the rich man so harsh?
   a. Because God is intolerant of self-indulgent people
   b. Because God has so much compassion for the poor
   c. Because God wanted him to use his resources more wisely
   d. Because God is jealous of other "gods" such as wealth

7. What does it mean to be "rich toward God"?
   a. Seeking first the Kingdom of God
   b. Placing God's priorities first
   c. Giving more of your money to the poor
   d. Using your abilities and resources to further God's Kingdom

8. If Jesus commented on America's view of wealth today, what do you think he would say?
   a. "Lifestyles of the rich and famous" is not the way to go
   b. You are grabbing for it all but missing the true meaning of life
   c. It is difficult to see the difference between Christian values and secular values.
   d. You have so much, but you are spiritually bankrupt

APPLY

STEP THREE: Wealth can be used in a variety of ways. For each of the following uses of wealth, place a "P" on the line if you think it is a positive use of wealth or an "N" if you think it is a negative use. Discuss your responses with your group.

____ to acquire power/influence
____ to help the needy
____ to take risks
____ to provide security
____ to indulge fantasies
____ to become famous
____ to seek public office
____ to make more money
____ to tithe to a church
____ to buy material goods
____ to impress others
____ to make friends and family happy
____ to support political ideology
____ to enjoy life
____ to give to charity
____ to increase self-esteem
____ to indulge your children
____ to intimidate others

OPTION 2

Epistle Study/Money Love

OPEN

STEP ONE: Start with the OPEN questions on page 20.

STUDY

STEP TWO: Read 1 Timothy 6:3–10 and discuss the questions below with your group. If you do not understand a word or phrase, check the Reference Notes on page 25.

3If anyone teaches false doctrines and does not agree to the
sound instruction of our Lord Jesus Christ and to godly teaching, 4he
is conceited and understands nothing. He has an unhealthy interest
in controversies and quarrels about words that result in envy, strife,
malicious talk, evil suspicions 5and constant friction between men of
corrupt mind, who have been robbed of the truth and who think that
godliness is a means to financial gain.
6But godliness with contentment is great gain. 7For we brought
nothing into the world, and we can take nothing out of it. 8But if we
have food and clothing, we will be content with that. 9People who
want to get rich fall into temptation and a trap and into many foolish
and harmful desires that plunge men into ruin and destruction. 10For
the love of money is a root of all kinds of evil. Some people, eager for
money, have wandered from the faith and pierced themselves with
many griefs.

1 Timothy 6:3–10 NIV

1. How does the love of money relate to the behavior described in verses 3, 4, and 5?

2. In what ways is a person who uses godliness for financial gain a false teacher?

3. What does "godliness with contentment" mean to you?

4. In what ways should the fact that "we can't take it with us" influence the way we live?

5. Why do you think most Americans are not content with just food, clothing, and shelter?

6. According to verses 9 and 10, what is wrong with pursuing wealth?

7. Is wealth inherently wrong? If so, why? If not, why not?

8. Why is the love of money, and not just money, "a root of all kinds of evil"?

REFLECT

STEP THREE: As time allows, discuss with your group your agreement or disagreement with the following statements.

- It is preoccupation with possession, more than anything else, that prevents men from living freely and nobly.

  — *Bertrand Russell*

- I have no complex about wealth. I have worked hard for my money, producing things people need. I believe that the able industrial leader who creates wealth and employment is more worthy of historical notice than politicians or soldiers.

  — *J. Paul Getty*

APPLY

STEP FOUR: Answer the following questions and share one of your responses with your group.

1. If you could reduce you financial commitments and simplify your lifestyle, would you do it? What is keeping you from doing it?

2. If you could put a little of your money into something you really believe in, where would you put it? What is keeping you from doing it?

REFERENCE NOTES

Summary . . . In this unit Paul summarizes the problem of false teachers and Timothy's role in dealing with them. In the process he provides some more details about the false teachers. It turns out that what motivates them is pride, a love of argument, and greed (vv. 3-5). However, what really ought to motivate us, Paul says, is "godliness with contentment" (vv. 6-10).

vv. 3-5 **. . .** False doctrine, Paul says, brings negative results. Those who have departed from the teaching of Jesus are people of dubious character who have brought disharmony into the church.

v. 3 **false doctrines . . .** Paul began this letter by pointing out that the problem in Ephesus was "false doctrine" (1:3). He now returns to this theme as he draws his letter to a close.

the sound instruction of our Lord Jesus Christ . . . This is their error. They have departed from the teaching of Jesus. This statement seems to indicate that early in the life of the church, the teachings of Jesus were collected and taught. The first Gospels were probably written around the time of this letter. However, whether this phrase refers to a written source or not, the point is that the origin of "sound instruction" is the Lord Jesus Christ (see also 1:10–11, 4:6).

v. 4 **he is conceited and understands nothing . . .** This is the first thing Paul says about these teachers. They are swollen with pride when, in fact, they are really quite ignorant. The NEB puts it well: they are "pompous ignoramus[es]"!

unhealthy interest . . . This is literally "being sick or diseased." This sort of "morbid craving" (as Bauer defines it) stands in sharp contrast to the sound (or "healthy") instruction of verse 3.

controversies . . . This is more than just "disputes." The word refers to a sort of idle speculation. They were preoccupied "with pseudo-intellectual theorizings" (Kelly).

quarrels . . . This is literally a "battle of words" which Paul sharply criticizes. He . . . paints in lurid colors the pride from which it springs, the spirit of anti-social bitterness and suspicion which it sows in the church, and the moral degeneracy which it eventually produces. The picture is a savage one, and although some of the details may be borrowed from conventional catalogues of vices, it suggests a concrete situation which excited Paul's distress and indignation (Kelly).

result in . . . Paul identifies two negative results of this sick preoccupation with word battles. First, it produces strife within the church, and second, it brings about a kind of corruption or decay to the minds of the teachers themselves.

envy . . . Controversy produces jealousy as people pick sides. (See Gal. 5:19–21; Rom. 1:29 where envy is said to be one of the fruits of the sinful nature.)

malicious talk, evil suspicions . . . This quarreling drives people to insult and question one another.

v. 5 **corrupt mind . . .** "Mind" refers not just to "the power of reason" but to one's whole way of thinking.

robbed of the truth . . . Such corruption results in the loss of the very truth of the gospel.

godliness is a means to financial gain . . . As Paul has hinted in 3:3 and 8, the bottom-line motivation of these false teachers is the money they make from their teaching. Paul does not consider it wrong for a person to be paid for teaching (see 5:17–18) but he is incensed when greed is the main motivation for ministry.

vv. 6–10 **. . .** Paul picks up on this problem of greed and says two things about it. First, godliness is to be much preferred to profit (vv. 6–8), and second, a love of money brings dire results.

v 6 **. . .** This verse stands in immediate contrast to the last words in verse 5, with a striking play on terms. *They* think godliness "is a way to become rich." Well (Gk., *de*, "indeed"), they are right. There *is* great profit (now used metaphorically) in godliness (*religion does make a person very rich*), provided it is accompanied by a "contented spirit" (Moffatt, Kelly), that is if one is satisfied with what one has and does not seek material gain (Fee).

contentment . . . This was a favorite word of the Stoic philosophers from whom Paul borrowed it. (Zeno, the founder of this philosophical school came from Tarsus, Paul's hometown.) This word refers to a person who is not impacted by circumstances. Such a person is self-contained and thus able to rise above all conditions. For Paul, however, this sort of contentment was derived from the Lord (see Phil. 4:11).

vv. 7–8 **. . .** There are two reasons why "godliness with contentment" brings great gain. First, at death people can take nothing with them, so why worry about material gain that has to be given up in the end anyway? Second, if people have the essentials in life, this should be enough.

vv. 9–10 **. . .** Paul ends by pointing out the dangers of riches. In these verses he chronicles the downward process that begins with the desire "to get rich." Such a desire leads into "temptation" which is, in turn, "a trap." The "trap" is the "many foolish and harmful desires" that afflict the greedy person. The end result is that such people are "plunge[d] . . . into ruin and destruction."

v. 9 **temptation . . .** Greed causes people to notice and desire what they might not otherwise have paid attention to.

v. 10 **For the love of money is a root of all kinds of evil . . .** Paul is probably quoting a well-known proverb in order to support the assertion he makes in verse 9 that the desire for money leads to ruin. This verse is often misquoted as "money is the root of all evil." While Paul clearly sees the danger of money, he is not contending that *all* evil can be traced to avarice.

some people . . . have wandered . . . Here is the problem. Some of the false teachers have given into the temptation to riches. They were probably once good leaders in the church but they got caught by Satan (4:1-2), became enamored with speculative ideas (6:3-5), and in the end were pulled down by their love for money.

SESSION 4
Success as Status

Even in a democratic society, status counts. Where we live, what kind of car we drive, and how we dress are important factors which help determine how we feel about ourselves and others. Some social commentators believe that it is an American myth that people can move easily up the class ladder. How we feel about our place and position in life can either lead to peace or perpetual dissatisfaction.

But what is true status? Is it living in the finest neighborhoods; having a powerful and influential job; or being brilliant and famous? Jesus' disciples debated the question of status and greatness. In the following studies, we will see both Jesus' and Paul's views on status and greatness.

OPTION 1

Gospel Study/Status Seekers

OPEN

STEP ONE: Answer the following questions and share your responses with your group.

1. We all have idols or heroes, especially as teenagers. Using the following categories, place the first name that comes to mind of someone you revered as a teenager. Compare names in your group. How many do you have in common?

___ book character	___ comic book character
___ TV character	___ movie star
___ pop music star	___ professional athlete
___ military hero	___ pastor/priest/rabbi
___ family member	___ other relative/friend

LEADER: IF YOU HAVE MORE THAN SEVEN AT THE MEETING SUBDIVIDE INTO GROUPS OF FOUR FOR GREATER PARTICIPATION (SEE BOX ON PAGE 6).

2. Who was your teenage idol or hero who stood out above the rest? Why that one? Over time, has that person measured up to your growing understanding of "success"? How so?

STUDY

STEP TWO: Read Mark 9:33-37 and discuss your responses to the following questions with your group

***33**They came to Capernaum. When he was in the house, he asked them, "What were you arguing about on the road?" **34**But they kept quiet because on the way they had argued about who was the greatest.*

***35**Sitting down, Jesus called the Twelve and said, "If anyone wants to be first, he must be the very last, and the servant of all."*

***36**He took a little child and had him stand among them. Taking him in his arms, he said to them, **37**"Whoever welcomes one of these little children in my name welcomes me; and whoever welcomes me does not welcome me but the one who sent me."*

Mark 9:33-37 NIV

1. Compared to your peers, siblings, and/or group members, in what six things (reading across columns 1, 2 and 3) are you "the greatest"? (Don't be afraid to brag a little or get an argument going.)

	1	2	3
a.	___ sleeping it off	___ sleeping late	___ being on time
b.	___ making snowmen	___ making up things	___ making out
c.	___ getting my way	___ getting away	___ getting in trouble
d.	___ doing homework	___ doing my thing	___ doing nothing
e.	___ tidying up	___ being tied down	___ tying up traffic
f.	___ keeping fit	___ making things fit	___ giving others fits

2. Why did the disciples keep quiet when Jesus asked them what they were arguing about?
   a. They were embarassed
   b. They knew he would scold them
   c. They were tired of listening to him preach at them
   d. They felt it was none of his business
   e. They knew they were wrong in arguing with each other

3. Why would the disciples even argue over who was the greatest?
   a. They believed that high status meant privilege
   b. They were just exhibiting their human nature
   c. They really didn't like each other
   d. They didn't understand what Christ had been teaching them

4. What did Jesus mean when he said that to be first, we must be the very last?
   a. The only status that matters is what God thinks of you
   b. By putting others first, you can manipulate them
   c. By serving others first, you are also serving God first
   d. When you serve others, they will step aside and let you go ahead
   e. When you serve others, you will inherit eternal life

5. Which of the following conventional wisdom contradicts Jesus' teaching?
   a. Only the strong survive
   b. You can have it all
   c. Look out for #1
   d. No guts, no glory

6. What does it mean to be a "servant of all"?
   a. Doing menial tasks for everyone else
   b. Following the example of Christ
   c. Allowing others to treat you poorly
   d. Maintaining an attitude which looks to serve others
   e. Considering others' interests over your own

7. Why did Jesus liken himself to a child?
   a. Because children have more admirable qualities than adults
   b. Because Jesus, like a child, is to be accepted just as he is
   c. Because children are loved and held in high esteem by God
   d. Because children are naturally humble and loving
   e. Because Jesus, like a child, should be accepted by faith

COMMENT: The context of this passage is important. Jesus has just predicted that he, as Messiah, will be rejected by the religious leadership in Israel. He will be killed, and then he will rise again (Mark 9:30–32). The disciples are literally unable to understand these words because Jesus' teaching is so different from what they understand about the Messiah. To them the Messiah will be a conquering hero who rids Israel of its enemies and establishes the world-wide reign of God.

APPLY

STEP THREE: Status-seeking can change a person's life. Answer the following question and discuss your responses with your group.

What are the most common changes one experiences when seeking status?

____ closer friendships
____ alienation of friends
____ selfishness
____ unselfishness
____ compromise
____ more integrity
____ stress
____ greater concern for others
____ competition
____ more time with family
____ less time with family
____ less concern for others
____ financial problems
____ excitement
____ more leisure
____ more work
____ less time with friends
____ more time with friends
____ increased self-esteem
____ family conflict
____ alienation of co-workers

OPTION 2

Epistle Study/Reverse Status

OPEN

STEP ONE: Start with the OPEN questions on page 28.

STUDY

STEP TWO: Read Philippians 2:5-11 and discuss the questions below with your group. If you do not understand a word or phrase, check the Reference Notes on page 32.

5Your attitude should be the same as that of Christ Jesus:
6Who, being in very nature God, did not consider equality with
God something to be grasped, 7but made himself nothing, taking the
very nature of a servant, being made in human likeness.
8And being found in appearance as a man, he humbled himself
and became obedient to death — even death on a cross!
9Therefore God exalted him to the highest place and gave him the
name that is above every name, 10that at the name of Jesus every
knee should bow, in heaven and on earth and under the earth, 11and
every tongue confess that Jesus Christ is Lord, to the glory of God
the Father.

Philippians 2:5-11 NIV

1. Have you ever had to reverse yourself from a stand you once took? Why? How did you feel at the time?

2. In what ways do we try to be equal with God?

3. Why would Christ choose to be a servant instead of exerting his power as God? What does this say about humility? About sacrifice?

4. If you had the opportunity to be God, what one thing would you do first?

5. In these verses, what do you learn about humility? About sacrifice?

6. Why does God reward the self-denying, servant behavior of Jesus?

7. How does God define status and success differently than society?

8. What do these verses say about achieving social status as a measure of success?

REFLECT

STEP THREE: As time allows, discuss with your group your agreement or disagreement with the following statements.

- Be not proud of race, face, place, or grace. — *Charles H. Spurgeon*

- God sends no one away empty except those who are full of themselves. — *Dwight L. Moody*

APPLY

STEP FOUR: Answer the following questions and share your responses with your group.

1. How is your view of status different from Jesus' view? Similar to Jesus' view?

2. What practical changes can you implement to make your view of status more closely conform to Jesus' view?

REFERENCE NOTES

Summary . . . From a theological point of view, this is the most important section in Philippians. Here Paul provides an amazing glimpse into the nature of Jesus Christ. Through Paul's eyes we see Jesus, the divine Savior who comes to his people in humility, not in power; we see the Lord of the universe before whom all bow choosing to die for his subjects; we see one who is in nature God, voluntarily descending to the depths (and becoming a servant) before he is lifted up to the heights (and assumes his kingship). This is a breathtaking glimpse that is made all the more astonishing because no one ever imagined that God would work his will in such a way. Who would have thought that God would act via weakness, not via power?

When Paul wrote these verses his main intention was not to make a theological point. Rather, his aim was to illustrate what self-sacrificing humility was all about. This is why he turns to the example of Jesus—he is the best illustration of a humble person that Paul knows. To demonstrate the humility of Christ, Paul quotes from an ancient Christian hymn about Jesus. Perhaps he composed the hymn himself. In quoting this hymn, Paul provides a fascinating glimpse into how the early Christians viewed Jesus. He also gives us one of the few existing examples of early church hymnology.

v. 5 **. . .** This is the transition verse between the exhortation of 2:1-4 and the illustration of 2:6-11. In it Paul states that the model for the sort of self-sacrificing humility he has been urging is found in Jesus.

vv. 6–11 **. . .** There is little agreement between scholars as to how this hymn breaks into verses or how it is to be phrased. However, one thing is clear: the hymn has two equal parts. Part one (verses 6–8) focuses on the self humiliation of Jesus. Part two (verses 9–11) focuses on God's exaltation of Jesus. In part one Jesus is the subject of the two main verbs, while in part two God is the subject of the two main verbs.

v. 6 **being . . .** This is not the normal Greek word for "being." "It describes that which a man is in his very essence, that which cannot be changed" (Barclay). This word also carries the idea of *pre-existence.* By using it Paul is saying that Jesus always existed in the form of God.

very nature . . . The Greek word used here is *morphe.* It is used twice by Paul in this hymn. He says that Jesus was "in *very nature* God" and that he then took upon himself "the *very nature* of a servant."

This is a key word in understanding the nature of Christ. Barclay defines *morphe* as "the essential form of something which never alters," in contrast to the word *schema* (which Paul uses in verse 7) which denotes outward and changeable forms. In other words, what Paul is saying is that Jesus Christ possessed the essential nature of God.

to be grasped . . . This is another rare word, used only at this point in the New Testament. It refers to the fact that Jesus did not have to "snatch" equality with God. Equality was not something he needed to acquire. It was his already, and thus he could give it away. Giving, not grasping, is what Jesus did.

vv. 7–8 **. . .** Paul uses four phrases to define what happened in the incarnation. Jesus "made himself nothing," he took "the very nature of a servant," he was made "in human likeness," and he was "found in appearance as a man." Each phrase gives a different glimpse into what Jesus became.

v. 7 **made himself nothing . . .** Instead of grasping godhood, Christ gave away what he had. This word means, literally, "to empty," or "to pour out until the container is empty." The way this is phrased indicates that this is something which Christ did voluntarily.

taking the very nature of a servant . . . Jesus gave up godhood and took on slavehood. From being the ultimate master, he became the lowest servant. He left ruling for serving. *Morphe* is used here again, indicating that Jesus adopted the essential nature of a slave. He did not "play act" being a slave for a time.

The use of the word *slave* here "emphasizes the fact that in the incarnation Christ entered the stream of human life as a slave, that is, as a person without advantage, with no rights or privileges of his own for the express purpose of placing himself completely at the service of all mankind" (Hawthorne).

being made . . . In contrast to the verb in verse 6 which stresses Christ's *eternal* nature, this verb points to the fact that at a *particular time* he was born in the likeness of a human being.

v. 8 **in appearance as a man . . .** The word translated "in appearance" is *schema* and denotes that which is outward and changeable—over against *morphe* which denotes that which is essential and eternal. In other words, Jesus was a true man but only temporarily. As Barclay puts it: "He is essentially divine; but he was for a time human. His mankind was utterly real, but it was something which passed: the godhead was also utterly real, but it is something which abides forever."

he humbled himself . . . This is the central point that Paul wants to make. This is why he offered this illustration. Jesus is the ultimate model of one who lived a life of self-sacrifice, self-renunciation, and self-surrender. Jesus existed at the pinnacle and yet descended to the very base. There has never been a more radical humbling. Furthermore, this was not something forced upon Jesus. Nor was it compelled by circumstances. This was voluntarily chosen by Christ.

obedient to death . . . The extent of this humbling is defined by this clause. Jesus humbled himself to the furthest point one can go. He submitted to death itself for the sake of both God and humanity. There was no more dramatic way to demonstrate humility.

death on a cross . . . For a Jew there was no more humiliating way to die. Jesus, who was equal to God, died like an accursed criminal. His descent from glory had brought him as low as one could go.

v. 9 **Therefore . . .** This word signals a whole new focus. In verses 6-8 it is Christ who is acting. The movement there is one of descent. But in verses 9-11, God is the prime actor and the movement is one of ascent. The self-humiliation of Jesus is followed by the God-induced exaltation of Jesus. Jesus descended to the depths and was raised to the heights. *This is the pattern of living that Paul is urging on the Philippians.* In Jesus one sees a fundamental principle of life at work—a principle that is true for everyone: the path to exaltation is via humiliation. To gain, one must give up.

exalted . . . The tense of this verb indicates that this exaltation took place by means of a single action, which is, of course, the resurrection/ascension of Jesus. From out of the depths of death he is given back life in its fullest form.

name . . . In the ancient world, a name was more than just a way of distinguishing one individual from another. It revealed the inner nature or character of a person. The name given the resurrected Jesus is the supreme name, the name above all names, because this is who Jesus is in his innermost being.

v. 10 **Jesus . . .** It is significant that the one before whom all will bow is Jesus, the man from Nazareth. The cosmic Lord is none other than the person who walked the roads of Palestine and talked to the people of Israel. He had a home town, a family, a trade, and disciples. The one before whom Christians will stand at the Last Judgment is not an anonymous Life Force, but the man of Galilee who has a familiar face.

bow . . . Everyone will one day pay homage to Jesus. This worship will come from all of creation—all angels (in heaven), all people (on earth), and all demons (under the earth).

v. 11 **Jesus Christ is Lord . . .** This is the climax of this hymn. This is the earliest and most basic confession of faith on the part of the church (see Acts 2:36; Romans 10:9; 1 Corinthians 12:3).

Lord . . . This is the name that was given to Jesus; the name that reflects who he really is (see verse 9). This is the name of God. Jesus is the supreme sovereign of the universe.

SESSION 5
Success as Happiness

If you have recently browsed the self-help section of your local bookstore, you are quite aware of the many "experts" who offer their road maps to happiness. Most of us seek happiness, but true happiness and contentment can be quite elusive. Often temporary happiness is achieved through positive events, new things, or "getting our own way."

Actually, what most of us seek is joy and not happiness. Happiness is dependent on external events; joy is an inner reality. Happiness is temporal; joy is eternal. Happiness is based on earthly circumstances; joy is based on spiritual realities. In the Gospel Study, you will have a chance to see what Jesus Christ had to say about the source of true joy in the Sermon on the Mount.

The Sermon on the Mount has been described as the "best definition of the mental attitude of someone who has turned over his or her life to God." The word "blessed" is often translated "happy" or "healthy." These mental attitudes may sound old-fashioned and even contradictory, but modern psychiatry is forcing the secular world to take another look at some of these rather shocking statements.

In the Epistle Study, you will have a chance to see how the Apostle Paul described his own mental attitude about life, written on his deathbed to the church in Philippi in modern-day Greece.

OPTION 1

Gospel Study/Happiness Is . . .

OPEN

STEP ONE: Answer the following questions and share your response with your group.

LEADER: IF YOU HAVE MORE THAN SEVEN AT THE MEETING SUBDIVIDE INTO GROUPS OF FOUR FOR GREATER PARTICIPATION (SEE BOX ON PAGE 6).

1. What time of your life would you describe as the happiest time? Why?

___ 0–9 years	___ 20–29 years	___ 50–59 years
___ 10–14 years	___ 30–39 years	___ 60–69 years
___ 15–19 years	___ 40–49 years	___ 70+ years

2. What moment from last week brings a smile to your face, joy in your heart and happy memories to mind?

STUDY

STEP TWO: Read Matthew 5:1-12 and discuss your response to the following questions with your group.

1 Now when he saw the crowds, he went up on a mountainside
and sat down. His disciples came to him, 2 and he began to teach
them, saying:
3 "Blessed are the poor in spirit, for theirs is the kingdom of
heaven.
4 Blessed are those who mourn, for they will be comforted.
5 Blessed are the meek, for they will inherit the earth.
6 Blessed are those who hunger and thirst for righteousness, for
they will be filled.
7 Blessed are the merciful, for they will be shown mercy.
8 Blessed are the pure in heart, for they will see God.
9 Blessed are the peacemakers, for they will be called sons of God.
10 Blessed are those who are persecuted because of
righteousness, for theirs is the kingdom of heaven.
11 "Blessed are you when people insult you, persecute you and
falsely say all kinds of evil against you because of me. Rejoice and be
glad, because great is your reward in heaven, for in the same way
they persecuted the prophets who were before you.

Matthew 5:1-12 NIV

1. What "blessed event" or "blessed person" in your family history do you still recall with great fondness, fervor and thanksgiving? For what "hoped-for event" in the near future do you seek God's blessing?

2. To what type of people is Jesus addressing this "sermon on the mount"?
   a. People who feel superior and competent
   b. Everyone, we all possess at least one of these characteristics
   c. Only his true followers in the first century
   d. Anyone who would listen
   e. Anyone with a bad attitude

3. Of the qualities listed in these verses, which one would you *least* like to have? Why? Of these, which would you *most* like to have? Why?

____ Being poor in spirit
____ Being mournful
____ Being meek
____ Being a peacemaker
____ Hungering and thirsting after righteousness
____ Being merciful
____ Being pure in heart

4. Why does Jesus hold these qualities in such high regard?
a. Because these qualities will make us happy
b. Because these qualities can counter evil
c. Because these qualities will help us get ahead
d. Because these qualities are marks of spiritual maturity

5. Why does Jesus put persecution in such a positive light?
a. Because if we are living according to Jesus' teachings, we will be persecuted
b. Because persecution will make us more aggressive
c. Because a "persecution complex" is spiritually healthy
d. Because persecution can lead to happiness
e. Because persecution will mature us spiritually

6. What is the relationship between persecution and joy?
a. Joy remains whether circumstances are positive or negative
b. Persecution can teach us to rely more on God—hence joy
c. Through persecution we can learn deeper meanings to life, such as joy
d. Joy is an emotional defense against persecution

7. Why is joy compatible with difficult circumstances while happiness usually is not?
a. Happiness is usually the temporary result of positive events
b. Joy is not dependent on external circumstances
c. Happiness is a much deeper emotion than joy
d. Joy is the result of our relationship with God

APPLY

STEP THREE: Answer the following questions and discuss your responses with your group.

1. Happiness and joy are not quite the same. For each of the following words, indicate whether each is more characteristic of happiness or joy by placing an "H" or a "J" respectively on the line. Discuss your responses with your group.

____ delight	____ security	____ elation
____ satisfaction	____ glee	____ bliss
____ ecstasy	____ gladness	____ peace
____ contentment	____ pleasure	____ confidence

2. What barriers are keeping you from experiencing joy?

3. What steps can you take to remove these barriers?

OPTION 2

Epistle Study/Employ Joy

OPEN

STEP ONE: Start with the OPEN questions on page 36.

STUDY

STEP TWO: Read Philippians 4:2-9 and discuss the questions below with your group. If you do not understand a word or phrase, check the Reference Notes on page 40.

[2]I plead with Euodia and I plead with Syntyche to agree with each other in the Lord. [3]Yes, and I ask you, loyal yokefellow, help these women who have contended at my side in the cause of the gospel, along with Clement and the rest of my fellow workers, whose names are in the book of life.

[4]Rejoice in the Lord always. I will say it again: Rejoice! [5]Let your gentleness be evident to all. The Lord is near. [6]Do not be anxious about anything, but in everything, by prayer and petition, with thanksgiving, present your requests to God. [7]And the peace of God, which transcends all understanding, will guard your hearts and your minds in Christ Jesus.

[8]Finally, brothers, whatever is true, whatever is noble, whatever is right, whatever is pure, whatever is lovely, whatever is admirable—if anything is excellent or praiseworthy—think about such things. [9]Whatever you have learned or received or heard from me, or seen in me—put it into practice. And the God of peace will be with you.

Philippians 4:2-9 NIV

1. First the positive: Where do you go, or what do you do, to get one hour's reprieve from and to recharge your worn-out batteries for facing the day's energy-draining conflicts?

2. Now the negative: In what ways have conflict and contention drained off energy from more constructive activity for you this week?

3. What does it mean to "rejoice in the Lord always"?

4. What perspectives and positions are necessary before one can "rejoice in the Lord always"?

5. According to verses 5, 6, and 7, what is the best therapy for anxiety?

6. Does the "peace of God" have an rational basis? If so, why? If not, why not?

7. What basis or criteria is used to determine what is true, noble, right, pure, lovely, admirable, excellent, and praiseworthy?

8. What is the motivation for making these characteristics part of your life?

REFLECT

STEP THREE: As time allows, discuss with your group your agreement or disagreement with the following statements.

- Happiness is not being pained in body or troubled in mind.

  — *Thomas Jefferson*

- God cannot give us happiness and peace apart from himself, because it is not there. There is no such thing.

  — *C.S. Lewis*

APPLY

STEP FOUR: Answer the following questions and share your responses with your group.

1. What barriers are keeping you from experiencing joy?

2. What steps can you take to remove these barriers?

3. What positive steps can you take to allow yourself to "rejoice in the Lord always?"

REFERENCE NOTES

Summary . . . Paul now pinpoints the specific problem confronting the Philippian church. Two of its leaders—Euodia and Syntyche—have had a falling out. And their disunity is threatening the unity of the whole church. (It is easy to imagine individuals lining up behind one or the other of these women so that factions develop.) In this unit, Paul first identifies the source of the disunity and then urges resolution of the problem. But he does not stop at that point. Then he launches into a series of admonitions, which if followed, will enable them to "stand firm in the Lord" (v. 1). He identifies those attitudes which enable people to cope successfully in difficult times. In the process Paul gives us one of the most profound lessons on the kind of mental state which promotes vital living. This unit completes Paul's teaching about joy.

v. 2 **plead . . .** This is a strong verb meaning "to exhort, to implore, to beg." The issue is so serious that Paul is willing to go on bended knee, as it were, to get it resolved. Paul uses this verb twice in verse 2 in order to underline the earnestness of his appeal. He also uses it twice to make it very clear that he is speaking to *both* of the contending parties. It is not a matter of one of them being in the wrong (and thus obliged to mend the split) while the other is in the right (and therefore without responsibility to work this out). Resolution will take work on the part of both women.

Syntyche/Euodia . . . Unlike most Greek women who remained in the background and had little to do with public life, Macedonian women were in every way as active and involved as the men. A businesswoman, Lydia, was Paul's first convert in Philippi. She organized the first house church there (see Acts 16:11-15, 40; 17:4, 12). These two women are, apparently, leaders in the present Philippian church. Their opinions are very important, so much so that their quarrel is threatening to split the church. Their unity is crucial to the unity of the whole body.

to agree . . . This is a far richer phrase in Greek than it is possible to translate into English. Paul is calling for agreement on more than just the cognitive level ("I agree with our ideas"). What he seeks is agreement in spirit and in attitude—a wholehearted, whole person sense of oneness. It will take this kind of agreement to heal the tragic split.

in the Lord . . . The only hope for this kind of unity to develop between these two women is found in the fact of their common commitment to Jesus. To be "in the Lord" is to emulate the mind set of the Lord. As Paul has already pointed out, this means that they are to forsake self-serving attitudes and instead embrace the self-giving attitude that the Lord demonstrated in his incarnation (2:1-11).

v. 3 **loyal yokefellow . . .** There has been much speculation about the identity of the person addressed here by Paul. He may simply be an unnamed colleague of Paul. Hawthorne feels that it is the whole church which is being called upon to help these women. Some suggest that the Greek word used here could be translated as if it were a proper name, *Syzygus,* in which case Paul would be reminding him to be true to his name ("loyal yokefellow") by assisting these women to resolve their differences.

contended . . . This word is used in the New Testament only here and in 1:27. It refers to strenuous athletic competition or to the hard work of fighting side by side as gladiators in an arena. These women were part of the team that sought to spread the gospel.

fellow workers . . . These women are numbered among the company of those like "Clement and the rest" who struggled side by side with Paul in the hard work of spreading the gospel. There is no hint—as some of the earlier commentators suggested—that Euodia and Syntyche merely worked among other women or somehow had a lesser role in ministry.

book of life . . . Cities like Philippi kept an official register with the names of all their citizens. Those who are members of the kingdom of heaven are likewise identified. What Paul is saying is that while his co-workers are too numerous to name in his letter, God is certainly aware of who they are.

v. 4 **Rejoice . . .** Paul returns to this central admonition which pervades the whole epistle. Here he concludes his teaching about joy by identifying how to rejoice even though the situation is difficult. In fact, "rejoicing" is the first of a series of attitudes that make it possible to cope successfully in hard times. If one is rejoicing, by definition, one cannot be despairing. Paul is not calling for people to rejoice *because* of the situation. Rather, it is the Lord who is the source and cause of rejoicing. In the following verses Paul describes how the Lord makes it possible for Christians to rejoice.

in the Lord . . . In the same way that Euodia and Syntyche can find agreement "in the Lord" (v. 2), so too, faith "in the Lord" makes joyfulness both realistic and possible, despite persecution and trouble.

always . . . In all situations.

v. 5 **gentleness . . .** Not only are the Philippians to rejoice, they are also to be "gentle" toward others. This is a difficult word to translate so as to capture its full meaning. This is the attitude of "graciousness" or "magnanimity" which is shown in situations when one could legitimately stand on one's "rights" and yet, for the sake of the other, does not insist on these rights.

The Lord is near . . . It is possible to rejoice and to act with gentleness because the Lord will return in the very near future and bring to an end all one's trials and difficulties. The Lord is "near" in a second sense as well. He is close to his children, via his Spirit, aiding them as they face these difficulties.

v. 6 **Do not be anxious . . .** The next command is negative. (The first two are positive—"rejoice" and "display gentleness.") They are to "stop worrying." This is not a command given lightly. The Philippians certainly had cause to worry; and Paul, who writes this command, is in prison. Yet to worry is to display a lack of confidence in God's care and in God's control over the situation (see Matthew 6:25-34).

prayer/petition/requests . . . Paul uses three synonyms in a row to describe the alternative to anxiety. Instead of worrying, a person ought to communicate directly with God and lay out before him all that is on his or her mind, confident that God will hear and respond.

with thanksgiving . . . When one is able to pray "with thanksgiving," anxiety is dealt with.

v. 7 **the peace of God . . .** This is the only time that this phrase is used in the New Testament. It must be distinguished from "peace with God," which comes as a result of justification by faith, and "peace from God," which is his gift to believers. The reference here is to the very peace of God himself. Peace, like love, is part of God's inner character and that which he himself experiences and displays. Amazingly, it is this peace which he offers to share with his children. It is this experience of the "peace of God" that makes it possible for Christians to rejoice in hard times.

transcends all understanding . . . Such peace can never fully be understood by human beings. It is the kind of peace which can never be figured out or produced by people themselves. It is that peace which relieves anxiety in a way quite beyond what people can do on their own.

guard . . . This is a military term. It describes a garrison of soldiers, such as those stationed at Philippi, whose job it is to stand watch over the city and protect it.

v. 8 **whatever is . . .** Paul lists a series of virtues—perhaps drawn from the teaching of the philosophers of his day (since these are unusual words not used in this sense elsewhere in Paul's writings). Paul urges them to reflect critically on ("think about") that which is *true* (sincerity and accuracy not only in thought and word, but in deed and attitude); *noble* (those majestic things which command respect and which lift up one's mind from the mundane); *right* (lit. "just," giving to God and others that which is their due); *pure* (in all spheres of life—ideas, actions, motives, etc.); *lovely* (a pleasant, friendly person who calls forth love from others); and *admirable* (that about which people think only good).

excellent . . . This is a word drawn from the vocabulary of Stoic philosophers. It refers to moral excellence.

praiseworthy . . . This refers to behavior that is universally praised. In other words, Paul is urging the Philippians to practice the kind of morality and behavior that would be commended even by their pagan colleagues. It is not surprising, therefore, that his list of virtues is not unique to Christianity but drawn from the best of pagan culture.

v. 9 **. . .** Yet there is a style of life which goes beyond pagan goodness. Ultimately their behavior ought to reflect the commandments of God which will at times be different from what popular culture commends.

learned/received/heard/seen . . . Paul identifies four sources of these commands. They were learned from the teaching of Paul (and others in the church); from the revelation of God (in the Old Testament and in the teachings of Jesus); and by what they hear and see in Paul's life.

SESSION 6
Success as Self-Fulfillment

"Self-fulfillment" is a rather recent concept. It has its modern origin in the writings of humanistic psychologists like Abraham Maslow and Carl Rogers. The concept of self-fulfillment or self-actualization reached full stride in the 1970's. If you peruse the magazine rack at your local supermarket, you will see the remnants of that decade in magazines like *SELF, Savvy Woman, US,* and *New Body.*

The proponents of the self-fulfillment doctrine place their faith in the ability of men and women to better themselves through self-improvement techniques. Most of the self-fulfillment approaches of today are based on the innate goodness of people. The following studies give us a different perspective on the source of true self-fulfillment.

However, Christians must not be too quick to dismiss altogether the concept of self-fulfillment because of the somewhat distorted way it is used in secular society. Christians, too, are called to a sort of self-fulfillment, although it is of a rather different kind than that spoken of in the popular magazines.

In the Gospel passage, Jesus teaches us that to find ourselves we must lose ourselves. In the Epistle passage, Paul states that true fulfillment is to be found in Christ.

OPTION 1

Gospel Study/Finding Yourself

OPEN

STEP ONE: Most of us seek a fulfilling life. From the following list, indicate where you look for fulfillment in your life. Share your responses with your group.

LEADER: IF YOU HAVE MORE THAN SEVEN AT THE MEETING SUBDIVIDE INTO GROUPS OF FOUR FOR GREATER PARTICIPATION (SEE BOX ON PAGE 6).

____ In my career/work	____ In friendships
____ In my marriage	____ In my children
____ In helping others	____ In making money
____ Through travel	____ Through exercise
____ Through education	____ In my spiritual life
____ Through psychotherapy	____ Through the arts

STUDY

STEP TWO: Read Matthew 16:21-28 and discuss your responses to the following questions with your group.

***21 From that time on Jesus began to explain to his disciples that
he must go to Jerusalem and suffer many things at the hands of the
elders, chief priests and teachers of the law, and that he must be
killed and on the third day be raised to life.***
***22 Peter took him aside and began to rebuke him. "Never, Lord!"
he said. "This shall never happen to you!"***
***23 Jesus turned and said to Peter, "Get behind me, Satan! You are
a stumbling block to me; you do not have in mind the things of God,
but the things of men."***
***24 Then Jesus said to his disciples, "If anyone would come after
me, he must deny himself and take up his cross and follow me. 25 For
whoever wants to save his life will lose it, but whoever loses his life
for me will find it. 26 What good will it be for a man if he gains the
whole world, yet forfeits his soul? Or what can a man give in
exchange for his soul? 27 For the Son of Man is going to come in his
Father's glory with his angels, and then he will reward each person
according to what he has done. 28 I tell you the truth, some who are
standing here will not taste death before they see the Son of Man
coming in his kingdom."***

Matthew 16:21-28 NIV

1. In what ways are Peter's actions similar to your own?
   a. I believe that I have some control over future events
   b. I act first then think later
   c. I do not like to hear bad news
   d. I step forward and take charge of situations
   e. In no way; I am not at all like Peter

2. Why did Jesus get so angry with Peter?
   a. Because Peter was being obnoxious
   b. Because Peter didn't understand what Jesus had said
   c. Because Peter was always interrupting Jesus
   d. Because Peter was interfering with God's divine plan

3. In what ways do God's concerns differ from man's concerns?
   a. God's concerns are universal and timeless; man's are not
   b. God is concerned with everything being perfect; man is not
   c. God is concerned with everyday details; man is not
   d. God is concerned with spiritual truth; man is not
   e. None of the above

4. Which one of the following best completes the statement, "If you really want to follow Jesus . . . ."?
   a. Put aside your creature comforts
   b. Get ready to play hardball
   c. First get your life in order
   d. Learn to make your personal desires secondary
   e. Get ready for a long, hard road

5. What is Jesus really saying in verse 25?
   a. If you live according to your desires, you'll mess up your life
   b. If you hang on too tightly to life, it will get away from you
   c. Follow Jesus and take your chances
   d. True self-fulfillment comes only through serving Jesus

6. What might be Jesus' response to the present-day desire to "have it all"?
   a. You may have it all, but you can't take it with you
   b. To have it all, you first need to follow me
   c. Are you willing to sell your soul to have it all?
   d. Obey God and you will have it all in eternity

APPLY

STEP THREE: Answer the following questions and discuss your responses with your group.

1. Which statement honestly represents your attitude toward self-fulfillment? Which one represents Jesus' view?
   a. Self-fulfillment is the highest calling of man
   b. Self-fulfillment is an illusion
   c. Self-fulfillment is an important personal goal
   d. Self-fulfillment is an invention of humanistic psychology
   e. Self-fulfillment comes through self-denial
   f. Self-fulfillment comes when we obey the Ten Commandments
   g. Self-fulfillment comes when you develop a plan and follow through on that plan
   h. Self-fulfillment comes when you let Jesus take control of your life

2. How do you reconcile the difference between your two views? How will you close the gap, in practice, this week, and thus find your true self?

OPTION 2

Epistle Study/ Completely Complete

OPEN

STEP ONE: Start with the OPEN question on page 45.

STUDY

STEP TWO: Read Philippians 1:15–26 and share your responses to the following questions with your group. If you do not understand a word or phrase, check the Reference Notes on page 49.

[15]It is true that some preach Christ out of envy and rivalry, but others out of good will. [16]The latter do so in love, knowing that I am put here for the defense of the gospel. [17]The former preach Christ out of selfish ambition, not sincerely, supposing that they can stir up trouble for me while I am in chains. [18]But what does it matter? The important thing is that in every way, whether from false motives or true, Christ is preached. And because of this I rejoice.

Yes, and I will continue to rejoice, [19]for I know that through your prayers and the help given by the Spirit of Jesus Christ, what has happened to me will turn out for my deliverance. [20]I eagerly expect and hope that I will in no way be ashamed, but will have sufficient courage so that now as always Christ will be exalted in my body, whether by life or by death. [21]For to me, to live is Christ and to die is gain. [22]If I am to go on living in the body, this will mean fruitful labor for me. Yet what shall I choose? I do not know! [23]I am torn between the two: I desire to depart and be with Christ, which is better by far; [24]but it is more necessary for you that I remain in the body. [25]Convinced of this, I know that I will remain, and I will continue with all of you for your progress and joy in the faith, [26]so that through my being with you again your joy in Christ Jesus will overflow on account of me.

Philippians 1:15–26 NIV

1. Some pastors can take a joke; several can dish it out. But others are cruelly hurt. In your social circles, what good-natured ribbing do you sometimes give your pastor? What fun does your pastor poke at himself or herself? What ill-will or Christian-bashing results by making ministers the butt of jokes in the media?

2. How do you explain that, despite abuses, the gospel of Christ is proclaimed?

3. If you were imprisoned for being a Christian, what do you think your attitude toward God would be?

4. What life-and-death dilemma does Paul face in verses 20-24?

5. What does Paul understand as ultimate fulfillment?

6. In what ways is joy related to a maturing Christian experience? (verses 25 and 26)

REFLECT

STEP THREE: As time allows, discuss with your group your agreement or disagreement with the following statements.

- Your life is without a foundation, if in any matter, you choose on your own behalf.

  — Dag Hammarskjold

- Fulfillment doesn't automatically happen as a result of linking up with the "right" person, job, or even ministry. Fulfillment . . . happens as a result of being in God's will.

  — Marilyn Olson

APPLY

STEP FOUR: Answer the following questions and share your responses with the group.

1. How did Paul find self-fulfillment?

2. What does Paul's statement mean to you: "To live is Christ and to die is gain"?

3. What helpful advice do you have for secular friends who are preoccupied with the search for self-fulfillment?

REFERENCE NOTES

Summary: . . . Beginning at 1:12 in his Epistle, Paul provides his friends with news about himself. He points to three positive outcomes as a result of his being in prison. First, the gospel is being noticed by all sorts of people who might otherwise not have heard it (v. 13). Second, the Christians in Rome have become bolder in their own proclamation (v. 14). And third, in the material we are looking at, he reports that even though some of the preaching that is going on springs from wrong motive, still the gospel is getting out (vv. 15-18).

Then in 1:18b-26 Paul talks about the future. He reflects on whether death or deliverance lies ahead for him. Paul displays a great deal of emotion as he contemplates this. His feelings go back and forth. One moment he is confident that he will be released. The next, he is worried that he might bring shame on himself or on Christ. He longs to be with Christ, but he also wants to go on living so that he will be a source of joy for the Philippians. On the other hand, it would be wonderful to lay down his burden and stand in the presence of the Lord that he has followed so long and served so faithfully. It is interesting to note that Paul is not at all reticent to express freely to his dear friends the full range of his emotions, including both his hopes and his fears.

v. 15 **some . . .** Although "most" (v. 14) of the brothers and sisters have been inspired by Paul's example and have become bolder in proclaiming the gospel, "some" have used his imprisonment as an opportunity to advance their own honor, prestige, or cause. With Paul in jail, he cannot oppose them. Notice, however, that Paul still considers these people to be "brothers." He may not like what they are doing nor their reasons for doing it, but he does not reject them as false teachers.

envy and rivalry . . . What motivates these people is some sort of grudge or hostility directed against Paul. They do not like him and want to hurt him by their preaching. What lay behind this animosity is not clear. Perhaps they looked on Paul in disdain because he was in jail, seeing this as a judgment from God against him. ("If God were really on his side, then he would not have allowed Paul to remain in prison," they might have reasoned.) Or maybe they were jealous of Paul's role as an apostle and saw this as a golden opportunity to advance their own position and authority.

good will . . . Paul identifies the motives of the majority of the Christians. They preach out of a feeling of "benevolence" (v. 15) and "love" (v. 16) toward him. These are "true" motives, as Paul says in verse 18a.

v. 17 **selfish ambition . . .** Paul identifies still another motive on the part of his rivals. The Greek word translated "selfish ambition" has an interesting history. It originally meant a "day laborer." It came to mean someone who did "sordid work." It was used in the political realm to describe a person who had a "partisan spirit." Eventually it came to refer to a relentless careerist who would do almost anything to promote his or her own advancement.

v. 18 **what does it matter . . .** There is about Paul a truly astonishing, magnanimous spirit which does not care about personal reputation or who gets the credit as long as the job gets done. He does not vilify those who use their preaching as a pretext to attack him. He continues to think of them as "brothers." It is this spirit that enables

Paul to cope, though in prison. His focus is not on the bad but on the good. He is not preoccupied with the misdeeds of these rivals. Instead, he rejoices over the fact that they preach Christ.

false motives . . . The three words by which Paul characterizes the motivation of his rivals—envy, rivalry, selfish ambition—are all words which he has used in other contexts to describe those actions and attitudes that are to be shunned by Christians (Romans 1:29; 2 Corinthians 12:20; Galatians 5:19-21; 1 Timothy 6:3-4).

Christ is preached . . . The one fact that makes it possible for Paul to accept this situation—and, in fact, to find positive value in it—is that whatever else might be said about these wrongly motivated brothers and sisters, their message still centers on Christ. They are preaching no new message (unlike those mentioned in 2 Corinthians 11:4 who preached "a Jesus other than the Jesus we preached.") Their message might not be quite the full Pauline version of the gospel, but it does maintain the centrality of Christ.

because of this I rejoice . . . This is an unexpected conclusion to Paul's report on his imprisonment. One might have expected an appeal that they pray for him in his difficult circumstances or that they work to get him released. This exclamation of joy is not how most people would sum up the experience of being in prison. But Paul has learned to see his circumstances in the light of God's plan; and so what matters is not how comfortable he is but whether the gospel is thriving—and since it is, Paul can rejoice!

vv. 18b-19 **. . .** In the previous unit (1:12-18a) Paul identified the first reason why he is able to rejoice even though he is in prison. His confinement has resulted in the gospel being preached even more widely. Here he identifies his second reason for rejoicing. He expects to be delivered from prison.

I will continue to rejoice . . . His own situation is far from ideal but Paul is able to "rejoice" because, as he showed in verses 12-18a, he sees the situation not from his own vantage point (his discomfort, his restriction of activity, his anxiety) but from the vantage point of God (the gospel is being preached more widely, thus people are being rescued from darkness). But there is something else that enables him to rejoice; his confidence that he will be delivered from this situation because of prayer and because of the Holy Spirit.

what has happened to me will turn out for my deliverance . . . This is the exact phrase that is used in Job 13:16 in the Greek version of the Old Testament. Quite likely Paul is consciously quoting from Job because Job's situation was so much like his own. This particular statement comes in the context of Job's reply to one of his "comforters." In this section Job professes his confident hope in God. In Job's case, God did make it right in the end and Paul is confident that this will be his experience also.

deliverance . . . There are three possible meanings for the word (*soteria* in Greek). First, it can be translated "salvation," and would, in this case, refer to acquittal on the day of judgment (see Romans 1:16; 10:10; 13:11). If Paul intends *soteria* to be understood as "salvation," then this verse means that his ultimate vindication will be in heaven. Whatever happens in Caesar's court, he knows that his final salvation is secure. Second, *soteria* can mean "good health," "wholeness," or "well-being." In this case, Paul's anticipation would be that everything will turn out, in the end, to have promoted his general welfare. Or, third, this word could be rendered "safety," "vindication," or "deliverance," in which case Paul would be anticipating that he will be released from prison. The latter seems the most likely meaning because in verses 25 and 26 he says: "I know that I will remain (i.e., not die), and I will continue with all of you . . ." And in 2:24 he tells them that he expects to visit them soon in Philippi. And yet Paul cannot be unaware that he may not be released—despite his confidence. In fact this may be one of the reasons why, in the following verses, he ruminates on the possibility of death.

v. 20 **eagerly expect . . .** This is "a picturesque word, denoting a state of keen anticipation of the future, the craning of the neck to catch a glimpse of what lies ahead" (Martin). It is a rare word, used only here and in Romans 8:19. Paul may even have coined this word himself.

ashamed . . . Paul is worried that he might disgrace either the gospel or himself as Christ's apostle by not giving a proper defense once he gets into court.

courage . . . What Paul desires is the courage to speak boldly during his trial.

by life or by death . . . By this phrase Paul simply means that his single goal is to bring praise to Christ.

vv. 21-24 . . . The phrase "by life or by death" seems to have caused Paul to reflect on these two realities. He is of two minds. Either option has value.

v. 21 **to live is Christ . . .** For Paul, his whole existence revolves around Christ. What he does, he does for Christ. He is inspired by Christ, he works for Christ, his sole focus in life is on Christ. He is a man with a single, all-consuming passion.

to die is gain . . . Precisely because Paul's sole ambition was to be "for Christ," his life has not been at all easy. In 2 Corinthians 11:23-29 he recounts a litany of difficulties that includes struggles, beatings, imprisonment, shipwreck, and hunger. In Philippians he mentions some of these same hardships (e.g., 1:29-30; 3:10; 4:14). With a load as heavy as this, it would not at all be a surprise that death might seem attractive to him. Death would be a way out from under it all. This idea of "death as a means of escape" was expressed by pagan writers of that era. Antigone said: "Whoever lives in as many ills as I—how does this one not get gain by dying" (quoted in Hawthorne). However, it is important to note that Paul does not himself in this passage state that he views death a means of escape. For Paul, the reason he can look at death in a favorable light is not negative (as an escape) but positive. Death will enable him to "be with Christ," the one around whom his whole existence revolves. In this way Paul parts company with his pagan counterparts when it comes to death.

v. 22 . . . Paul does not know which path is best: "To die is gain" but release from prison—which he anticipates—will give him the opportunity to do further missionary work.

v. 23 **to depart and be with Christ . . .** For Paul, death would be the way to deepen his union with Christ. Death is the door into the presence of Christ. Death is the path to *reunion* with the one with whom he is already *in union.* Death for Paul is not so much an escape from hardship as it is an entrance into joy.

better by far . . . So strong is Paul's desire to be with Christ that he uses a triple adverb as an emphatic superlative to describe his preference. When translated literally this phrase means "much rather better."

SESSION 7
Success as Service

In 1961, President John F. Kennedy signed an executive order which brought the Peace Corps into existence. The purpose of the Peace Corps is to provide humanitarian services to people of developing nations. In the 1960's this ideal inspired many young and not-so-young Americans to volunteer their services. Today, this spirit of service is less apparent in our society. In fact, service is given a low priority. (Service occupations are traditionally among the lowest paying jobs.)

But Jesus did not view service the same way. In the Gospel Study, we see that he exemplified the role of a servant—and prods us to do the same. The Apostle Paul echoes a similar theme in the Epistle passage from Galatians. In both passages, service and servanthood are elevated when framed in a spiritual perspective. This is where true success lies.

OPTION 1

Gospel Study/Self Service

OPEN

STEP ONE: What do you look for in a leader of your company, your church, or your small group? Is it any different than what you would look for in hiring someone in the traditional service occupations? To find out, rank order from 1-10 (in the space at the left) these qualities in order of their importance for a *leader*. Then go back and rank order (in the space at the right) those qualities you would look for in a *servant*. What does a comparison of your rankings tell you?

LEADER: IF YOU HAVE MORE THAN SEVEN AT THE MEETING SUBDIVIDE INTO GROUPS OF FOUR FOR GREATER PARTICIPATION (SEE BOX ON PAGE 6).

______ courteous: always kind, no job too menial ______

______ motivational: able to inspire confidence in others ______

______ good-humored: wears a smile, makes others smile ______

______ courageous: willing to take risks, even fail ______

______ professional: skilled and knowledgeable ______

______ easy-going: able to complement the hard-drivers ______

______ aggressive: dedicated to reaching goals ______

______ pragmatic: practical and resourceful in helping ______

______ unselfish: deferential, puts others first ______

______ initiative: sets the example by going first ______

STUDY

STEP TWO: Read John 13:1–17 and discuss your responses to the following questions with your group.

1It was just before the Passover Feast. Jesus knew that the time
had come for him to leave this world and go to the Father. Having
loved his own who were in the world, he now showed them the full
extent of his love.

2The evening meal was being served, and the devil had already
prompted Judas Iscariot, son of Simon, to betray Jesus. 3Jesus knew
that the Father had put all things under his power, and that he had
come from God and was returning to God; 4so he got up from the
meal, took off his outer clothing, and wrapped a towel around his
waist. 5After that, he poured water into a basin and began to wash his
disciples' feet, drying them with the towel that was wrapped around
him.

6He came to Simon Peter, who said to him, "Lord, are you going
to wash my feet?"

7Jesus replied, "You do not realize now what I am doing, but later
you will understand."

8"No," said Peter, "you shall never wash my feet."

Jesus answered, "Unless I wash you, you have no part with me."

9"Then, Lord," Simon Peter replied, "not just my feet but my
hands and my head as well!"

10Jesus answered, "A person who has had a bath needs only to
wash his feet; his whole body is clean. And you are clean, though not
every one of you." 11For he knew who was going to betray him, and
that was why he said not every one was clean.

12When he had finished washing their feet, he put on his clothes
and returned to his place. "Do you understand what I have done for
you?" he asked them. 13"You call me 'Teacher' and 'Lord,' and rightly
so, for that is what I am. 14Now that I, your Lord and Teacher, have
washed your feet, you also should wash one another's feet. 15I have
set you an example that you should do as I have done for you. 16I tell
you the truth, no servant is greater than his master, nor is a
messenger greater than the one who sent him. 17Now that you know
these things, you will be blessed if you do them.

John 13:1–17 NIV

1. In the past year, do you suppose you are a debtor or a creditor when it comes to doing favors for one another? Why is that? To whom do you have the biggest outstanding IOU?

2. Why do you think Jesus chose the Passover Feast to show favor to his disciples?
   a. He knew he didn't have much time left on earth
   b. He was more emotional during the Passover season
   c. He wanted to equate his sacrificial love with God's love in delivering the Jews from Egypt
   d. He realized that the disciples were more receptive to spiritual teaching during this religious celebration

3. In what ways is Judas Iscariot's betrayal of Jesus the opposite of love, humility, and service?
   a. He was only looking out for #1
   b. He was being deceitful and dishonest
   c. He placed his desires above the needs of Jesus and the others
   d. He valued personal gain most

4. During Jesus' time humility was seen as a weakness. Why did Jesus perform the humiliating act of footwashing on his disciples?
   a. He wanted them to learn and follow his example of serving others
   b. He wanted to convey that he was a weak leader
   c. He wanted to show that humility and service were signs of strength and not weakness
   d. He was visually illustrating why he had come to earth

5. Why didn't Jesus do what Peter had requested?
   a. Jesus realized that Peter didn't know what was happening
   b. Jesus was tired of Peter's impulsiveness
   c. Jesus was anxious to get the footwashing finished
   d. Jesus knew exactly what he wanted to teach his disciples

6. In what ways did Jesus establish his authority to do what he did?
   a. He took control of the situation
   b. He squelched all opposition
   c. He appealed to a higher authority
   d. He reminded them who he was—their Teacher and Lord

7. What was Jesus trying to teach his disciples by his actions?
   a. That it is important to be humble
   b. That he was no better than they were
   c. That successful living is found in serving God and others
   d. That serving others will only result in humiliation

8. Why did Jesus want his disciples to be servants?
a. Because serving others is an expression of love
b. Because serving others would "turn the world upside down"
c. Because serving others would frustrate the Jewish leaders
d. Because serving others would exemplify God's new order

APPLY

STEP THREE: If you were called upon to serve others, which *two* of the following areas of service would you choose. Discuss your choices with your group.

____ American Red Cross	____ School board
____ World Vision	____ Short-term mission
____ Meals on Wheels	____ Long-term mission
____ Local government	____ Consumer advocacy
____ VISTA	____ Neighborhood anti-crime
____ Feeding/clothing the poor	____ Armed Forces
____ Hospital visitation	____ Shut-in visitation
____ Big Brother	____ Historical Society
____ Wildlife preservation	____ Orphanage
____ Sunday School class	____ Anti-nuclear movement
____ Amnesty International	____ Counseling abused women
____ Neighborhood organization	____ Church board
____ Art council	____ Housing street people
____ Peace Corps	____ Anti-abortion counseling
____ Boy Scouts/Girl Scouts	____ Church choir
____ Adoption agency	____ Handicapped assistance
____ Nursing Home visitation	____ Other ____________________
____ Habitat for Humanity	

OPTION 2

Epistle Study/Full Service

OPEN

STEP ONE: Start with the OPEN question on page 54.

STUDY

STEP TWO: Read Galatians 5:13–26 and share your responses to the following questions with your group. If you do not understand a word or phrase, check the Reference Notes on page 59.

***13You, my brothers, were called to be free. But do not use your
freedom to indulge the sinful nature; rather, serve one another in
love. 14The entire law is summed up in a single command: "Love your
neighbor as yourself." 15If you keep on biting and devouring each
other, watch out or you will be destroyed by each other.***

***16So I say, live by the Spirit, and you will not gratify the desires of
the sinful nature. 17For the sinful nature desires what is contrary to
the Spirit, and the Spirit what is contrary to the sinful nature. They are
in conflict with each other, so that you do not do what you want. 18But
if you are led by the Spirit, you are not under law.***

***19The acts of the sinful nature are obvious: sexual immorality,
impurity and debauchery; 20idolatry and witchcraft; hatred, discord,
jealousy, fits of rage, selfish ambition, dissensions, factions 21and
envy; drunkenness, orgies, and the like. I warn you, as I did before,
that those who live like this will not inherit the kingdom of God.***

***22But the fruit of the Spirit is love, joy, peace, patience, kindness,
goodness, faithfulness, 23gentleness and self-control. Against such
things there is no law. 24Those who belong to Christ Jesus have
crucified the sinful nature with its passions and desires. 25Since we
live by the Spirit, let us keep in step with the Spirit. 26Let us not
become conceited, provoking and envying each other.***

Galatians 5:13–26 NIV

1. When you were "coming of age," what did "freedom" mean to you? Free to do what? Free from what?

2. What does it mean to be "free" in Christ?

3. In what ways is this freedom in Christ potentially dangerous?

4. How does loving your neighbor relate to loving yourself?

5. What are some examples of how human desires conflict with spiritual truth?

6. When human desires conform to God's desires, what changes take place?

7. If the "fruit of the Spirit" became normal behavior, in what ways would the world be a different place to live?

8. How does the fruit of the Spirit become a reality in a person's life?

REFLECT

STEP THREE: As time allows discuss with your group your agreement or disagreement with the following statements.

- There is no higher religion than human service. To work for the common good is the greatest creed.

  — *Albert Schweitzer*

- The service that counts is the service that costs.

  — *Howard Hendricks*

APPLY

STEP FOUR: Answer the following questions and share your responses with your group.

1. How do the fruits of the Spirit enable you to love others?

2. How do you respond to the statement that for the Christian, success is found in service?

3. What key lessons have you learned about success from this series of Bible studies?

4. What topic would you like to tackle next as a group?

REFERENCE NOTES

Summary: . . . The law of God is summed up in the so-called Great Commandment which Paul quotes in verse 14. However, this sort of love is hampered by those who live according to the desires of the sinful nature (some of which he identifies in verses 19-21). On the other hand, love is fostered by those who live according to the Spirit. In verses 22-25, Paul identifies the attitudes and activities that characterize the fruit of the Spirit.

v. 13 **free. But . . .** What Paul has written about freedom from the law could be misunderstood to be a license to indulge all one's appetites, and certainly he does not mean that. So he begins this new section on Christian living by examining the use of freedom. What Paul is calling for is responsible freedom, which, as he says is the freedom to serve others in love.

freedom . . . Christian freedom stands between the one extreme of legal bondage—life lived within a web of requirements (5:1)—and the other extreme of unbridled indulgence—life lived without regard to any rules. Paul has said that no one can be truly free until Christ takes away his/her burden of guilt (Christ frees a person from the power of the law). Now he will show that one also needs to be freed from the power of sinful desires, which comes by the infilling of the Holy Spirit.

the sinful nature . . . The self-serving, self-seeking, self-indulgent aspect of human nature—see vv. 19–21 for a partial list of its works.

serve . . . Literally "serve as slaves." The only form of slavery that is compatible with freedom is self-giving to others.

v. 15 . . . By means of the rather vivid image of a pack of wild animals tearing one another to pieces, Paul warns here against this particular "work of the flesh." Apparently the Judaizers had provoked strife and controversy in the Galatian church.

v. 16 . . . Having warned against losing one's freedom by submitting to circumcision (5:2–3), Paul now warns about losing freedom by submitting to sinful desires.

live by the spirit . . . Literally "walk" by the spirit; i.e., let the way you live, your conduct, be directed by the Holy Spirit. It is the Holy Spirit, not the law, that will bring about a moral life style. See Romans 8:5–9; 12–13.

v. 17 . . . Two principles are at war in the Christian's life. The Spirit moves a person in one direction, the sinful nature in the opposite. "But the believer is not the helpless battle—group of two opposing forces. If he yields to the flesh, he is enslaved by it, but if he obeys the prompting of the Spirit, he is liberated" (Bruce).

v. 18 . . . The Spirit is as opposed to the *law* as to the *sinful nature* (vv. 16–17). To be led by the Spirit enables a person to resist sinful desire. To be under law, however, gives a person no protection at all against such inner cravings. "To be led by the Spirit brings simultaneous deliverance from the desire of the flesh, the bondage of the law, the power of sin" (Bruce).

led . . . The word is used elsewhere to describe a shepherd leading sheep, a soldier escorting a prisoner to jail, or a wind driving a ship. The focus is on the initiative of the Spirit. However, in vv. 16 and 25, by the use of the phrase "live by the Spirit," the other side of the issue is pointed out: simultaneously the Christian has an active part to play in the sort of life he/she lives (Stott).

v. 19 **acts of the sinful nature . . .** "To" illustrate specifically the sort of life-style that emerges when the "flesh" (sinful nature) is allowed its sway, Paul produces a representative list of vices.

sexual immorality . . . Porneia (from which "pornography" is derived) refers to sexual irregularity in general and contact with prostitutes specifically.

impurity . . . This word includes misuse of sex but is wider in scope, involving *impurity* of both a moral and a ritual kind (doing that which makes one unfit to come before God).

debauchery . . . The public practice of vice without restraint and without caring what others know or feel about it.

v. 20 **idolatry . . .** The worship of any idol, be it a carved image of God (a statue) or an abstract substitute for God (a status symbol). Such an idol is identified when a person, faced with a choice, will follow its leading. Money, for example, becomes an idol when a person will do anything to gain it.

witchcraft . . . *Pharmakeia* is literally "the use of drugs," which was often associated with the practice of sorcery.

hatred . . . The underlying political, social and religious hostility which drives apart individuals and communities.

discord . . . Contention and quarreling.

jealousy . . . In a different context this word could be translated "zeal." But zeal can degenerate into jealousy (i.e. the illegitimate desire to have what another has) and this is the meaning of the word here.

selfish ambition . . . The word originally meant "work done for pay." It then came to refer to a person who sought political office for his own purposes, and finally came to carry the sense of one who works only for his own good and not for the benefit of others.

dissension . . . Literally "a standing apart."

factions . . . *Hairesis* (from which *heresy* is derived) means the party spirit which emerges amongst those with a common viewpoint that causes them to regard those who differ as enemies.

v. 21 **envy . . .** A grudging spirit that hates to see another prosper.

drunkenness . . . In the first century, diluted wine was drunk regularly by all ages, but drunkenness was not common and was condemned because it was thought to turn a person into a beast.

orgies . . . Revelry or carousing; unrestrained celebration that degenerates from joyousness into license.

not inherit . . . "While good deeds in themselves do not admit one to the kingdom, evil deeds of this type mentioned certainly exclude one" (Bruce). While the Christian has assurance of God's forgiveness, the issue here is not sins into which one falls but sin as a life-style. This is evidence of a life not controlled by the Spirit and therefore the implication is that such a person has not been born from above and become a child of God.

kingdom of God . . . Here this phrase signifies the future kingdom of God in the age to come when God's children will realize their inheritance. As for now, the presence of the Holy Spirit is the first installment of that inheritance, i.e. that which guarantees the rest.

vv. 22-23 **fruit of the Spirit . . .** In contrast to the "works of the flesh" is the fruit of the Spirit, those traits which characterize the child of God. Again the list is representative and not exhaustive.

v. 22 **love . . .** *Agape.* In contrast there is *eros* (sexual love); *philios* (warm feelings to friends and family); and *storge* (family affection). None of these adequately describe the selfgiving, active benevolence that is meant to characterize Christian love, hence the repeated use in the New Testament of *agape*—a relatively uncommon word redefined by Christians to bear this meaning.

joy . . . The source of joy is God (Rom. 5:11).

peace . . . The prime meaning of this word is not negative: "an absence of conflict" but positive: "the presence of that which brings wholeness and well-being."

patience . . . The ability to bear with people for a long time. The idea is of steadfastness and endurance.

kindness, goodness . . . Related words, but whereas *kindness* means the sort of response that is gentle and sweet, *goodness* includes the ability to rebuke and discipline when necessary. As Trench points out, Jesus demonstrated *goodness* when he drove the money-changers from the temple, but *kindness* to the harlot that annointed his feet.

faithfulness . . . Reliability, trustworthiness.

gentleness . . . According to Aristotle, this is the virtue that lies between excessive proneness to anger and the inability to be angry; it implies control of oneself.

self-control . . . This is control of one's sensual passions rather than control of one's anger (as in gentleness).

there is no law . . . While it is possible to legislate certain forms of behavior, one cannot command love, joy, peace, etc. These are each gifts of God's grace. With this list of qualities one moves into a whole new realm of reality, well beyond the sphere of law.

v. 24 **have crucified the sinful nature . . .** It is via the cross that a person dies to the power of the law (2:19). Here Paul indicates that in the same way a person also dies to the power of his/her sinful nature. The verb indicates that this is not something done *to* the Christian but *by* the Christian. The Christian actively and deliberately has repented of (turned away from) the old wayward patterns of life.

v. 25 **live by the Spirit . . .** In the same way that the death of the ego (the "I" principle) is replaced by the mind of Christ (2:20), Paul indicates that the death of the sinful nature is replaced by the life of the Spirit.

let us . . . Having just indicated that the Christian does live by the power of the Spirit, Paul, in characteristic fashion, balances off the indicative ("This is the way things are") with an imperative ("Now you do this"). The Christian life involves both action by God and by people.

keep in step . . . Walk in line, let the Spirit direct the path that is chosen.

v. 26 **conceited . . .** To boast when there is nothing to boast about!

provoking . . . The word was used to describe a challenge to an athletic contest or to combat.

SUGGESTED READING

From a Christian perspective:

The Success Fantasy, Anthony Campolo, Wheaton, IL: Victor Books, 1980.

Failure: The Backdoor to Success, Erwin W. Lutzer, Chicago: Moody Press, 1976.

While Walking on Water . . . I Sank, Joe Lomuscio, San Bernadino, CA: Here's Life America Publishers, 1986.

The Success Factor: Discovering God's Potential Through Reality Thinking, Archibald D. Hart, Englewood Cliffs, NJ: Revell, 1984.

From a secular perspective:

The Success Syndrome: Hitting Bottom When You Reach the Top, Steven Berglas, New York: Plenum Press, 1986.

Modern Madness: The Emotional Fallout of Success, Douglas LaBier, Reading, MA: Addison-Wesley Publishing Co., 1986.